Introduction ....

33 Great Balcony Garden Ideas & DIY Balcony Garden Guide 3

   Why Have a Balcony Garden? 3

      Balcony Gardening vs Terrace Gardening 3

   Balcony Garden Best Ideas for Inspiration 4

      Small Balcony Garden Ideas 4

      Herb Garden on Balcony Ideas 10

      Balcony Container Gardening Ideas 14

      Vegetable Gardening on Balcony Ideas 18

      Apartment Balcony Garden Ideas 23

      Home Balcony Gardening Ideas 29

      Vertical Garden Ideas for Balcony 33

   Best Balcony herbs and Vegetables 40

      Best Veggies for Your Balcony Garden 40

      Best Flowers for Your Balcony Garden 40

   How to Make a DIY Balcony Garden 41

      Step one – Consider Your Space 41

      Step two – Choose Your Design 41

      Step 3 – Choose Your herbs 41

      Step 4 – Select Your Planters 41

      Step 5 – Add Some Furniture 41

      Step 6 – Safety and Maintenance 41

   Balcony Garden Frequently Asked Questions 42

      What vegetables possibly grown on a balcony? 42

      What do I must for a balcony garden? 42

      How do I build a small balcony garden? 42

   Less Is More 42

Introduction

In this book, you will see 33 balcony ideas.

If you have a balcony, then imagine how pleasant it is to go out, look at the sky and let the scent of nature breathe.

Besides, not everyone lives in the countryside with large backyards. So a green balcony is a perfect solution for the apartment-dwelling gardening buff.

Plus, in the midst of a concrete jungle, a bit of nature may have therapeutic and calming effects.

33 Great Balcony Garden Ideas & DIY Balcony Garden Guide

When you hear the word "garden," what's the first image that comes to mind? A green oasis in your front or back yard? A bed of flowers adjoining a lush lawn? A plot of land for vegetables and fruits? Probably not a **balcony garden**!

But have you ever thought of bringing all of that and more to your balcony? And why not? You'll add railing planters, hanging baskets, freestanding pots, trellises, and even crates and pallets to transform your balcony into your dream garden.

What's more, you'll culture anything and everything in your balcony garden so long as your herbs get enough sunshine, water, and love.

So are you ready to **Make your own green balcony**? Put on your gardening boots, take up your trowel, and read on for some awesome balcony garden ideas.

Why Have a Balcony Garden?

For starters, a little greenery never hurt anyone. Balconies are easy to transform into green spaces and even easier to take care of. Blooming all summer long, a balcony garden may add to the overall charm of your house.

A balcony garden can also work as a natural climate cooler, reduce pollution, and block high-frequency noise. So this seems there are many great reasons for you to start gardening on your balcony.

Balcony Gardening vs Terrace Gardening

Both balcony and terrace gardening have the same approach—making the most of small garden spaces. however while balcony gardens are more compact, terrace gardens are larger and may cover the entire roof space.

Balcony gardens are also generally sheltered or enclosed. On the other hand, terrace gardens are more open and climatey. Thus, balcony gardens are not as versatile as terrace gardens.

On the plus side, balcony gardens are more accessible as they're often connected to indoor living spaces like the bedroom or kitchen.

Balcony Garden Best Ideas for Inspiration

A balcony is perhaps one of the most overlooked gardening spaces. however you'll simply make this into a therapeutic and blooming garden.

Culture perennials, ornamental herbs, shrubs, trees, and even herbs and vegetables in your balcony. As you're happy with your space, throw in a couple of chair to enjoy a cup of afternoon tea, read a book, or take a nap.

From an apartment to a container or vertical balcony yard, here's a list of the best ideas you'll take inspiration from.

Small Balcony Garden Ideas

Supposing your balcony is small or narrow, or simply can't hold a full-sized yard, don't worry. You'll simply get started on a small balcony garden with these awesome ideas.

1. Rail Balcony Garden Bed

Not sure how to greenify a narrow and long balcony without shrinking this further? Go for railing planters. You'll fix them on the rails or hang them employing metal hooks.

Culture seasonal blooms or ornamental herbs in your planters. They can add a good pop of color to your balcony without making this look too crowded.

2. Minimalist Freestanding Container

Who says minimalists can't rock balcony gardens? Introduce a couple of freestanding planters in varied shades and shapes to your balcony, and voila!

Culture ornamental herbs like paradise palm and umbrella herb for the right dose of greenery.

Idea: employ faux lawn grass for added effect and define this with white river rocks.

3. Deck-Style Balcony Garden

For something offbeat, turn your balcony into a miniature deck. employ wooden planks or deck tiles like in the image below. Add faux grass and pebbles to draw eyes.

Make employ of the railing to hang planters. A pallet wall may also be used to hang potted herbs.

Advice: Turn gardening equipment like boots, shovels, hoes, and watering mays into decor items.

4. Balcony Floral Oasis

Even supposing your balcony space is scarce, you'll simply enjoy a floral garden. employ hanging planters and pots that possibly hooked to the railings.

Culture petunias, geraniums, and clematis to make your space look like it's straight out of an Italian rom-com.

5. Secret Rose Garden

Make a retreat you'll escape to in your own balcony. How? With roses! They look absolutely gorgeous and can make your space fragrant all summer long.

While roses may simply be grown in colorful pots, you'll also allow the climbing varieties to spread across your balcony.

Herb Garden on Balcony Ideas

Imagine having fresh and fragrant basil, rosemary, lemongrass, and mint waiting to be picked and used in your kitchen. Tempting, isn't it? What's even better is that you'll get started on a herb garden in your balcony.

Most herbs do well in small spaces and are not as fussy as flowering or ornamental herbs. Plus, they'll make your balcony scent great!

Below are some balcony herb garden ideas you'll take inspiration from.

6. Terra Cotta Balcony Herb Garden

Culture herbs like dill, rosemary, and basil in terra cotta planters. however why terra cotta? Well, clay planters look attractive and are porous, which means that you don't have to worry about overwatering your herbs.

Advice: *You'll hook the planters to the balcony railing or place them on the ground.*

7. Tin May *Planters*

Use old or unused tin mays to make classy planters for your balcony. Nail holes in them and fasten them to the railing employing zip ties.

Small tin mays possibly used to herb shallow-rooted herbs like basil and thyme while parsley and lemongrass would must larger mays.

Advice: Line the sides of your balcony with these planters to keep the floor uncluttered.

8. Metal Stclimatecase Stand

Set up your balcony herb garden in a multi-level metal stand. These stands come in different sizes and are highly durable, too.

Not only can they allow you to culture a variety of herbs in limited space, however also help display them lovelinessly.

9. Wood DIY Planter Box

Make your own planter box employing scraps of wood from useless pallets. As your planter is ready, fill this with soil. Culture herbs like mint, basil, parsley, and oregano in your planter.

Idea: employ tiny chalkboards to mark different herbs. This way, you'll famous which herbs you have in your little garden.

10. Wooden Crate Planters

Upcycle old wooden crates to hold your herb garden. These planters have a rustic, country vibe and don't take up too much room.

You'll also raise them off the ground employing wooden legs. This way, you wouldn't have to stoop while collecting fresh herbs.

Balcony Container Gardening Ideas

Container gardens are one more great way to save space in your balcony. You'll employ fancy plastic, terra cotta, and wooden planters. however why limit yourself? Upcycle metal buckets, pallets, tin mays, and crates, too.

Here are some container gardening ideas you'll take inspiration from.

11. Multi-Colored Metal Buckets

Turn up the heat in your balcony garden with colorful metal buckets. Go for bold hues—pink, red, orange, and blue. These planters can look fancy even in winters when your herbs turn bare.

Plant dahlias, lavenders, roses, and pansies as they are easy-to-care-for and vibrant.

12. Trellis Fclimatey Plater

A wooden trellis to hang pots is too loveliness to not include in your balcony. You'll fasten planters of varied sizes to this and get gardening.

Now include a small fclimatey house and some fclimatey lights to your arrangement to invite pixies to your balcony.

Advice: Place a café table in your balcony where you'll escape to whenever you please.

13. Hanging Clay Pots

For a striking visual element, hang terra cotta pots from the ceiling of your balcony. Make a chain of pots supposing you want to make the most of your vertical space.

This way, your balcony space can not shrink further. Plus, you'll be able to enjoy the bright seasonal blooms.

14. Urn Planters

For a balcony garden that is sure to steal the show, bring in urn planters. Paint them with striking colors and arrange them in clean rows.

Such planters have an offbeat look and may make your balcony garden stand out.

Idea: Culture moss roses in shades of magenta and yellow like in the photo below.

Vegetable Gardening on Balcony Ideas

To culture vegetables at home, you don't must a large backyard. Your balcony space is quite enough. Given the right care, you'll simply reap the "veggies" of your hard work.

Below are some wonderful vegetable balcony gardens ideas for you:

15. Garden Vegetable Basket

Plastic baskets are perfect to get started on balcony vegetable gardens. They are space-saving, durable, lightweight, and generally portable. Fill them with good potting or planting mix.

Advice: herb easy-to-culture greens like lettuce, spinach, kale, cabbage, and coriander in your baskets.

16. Crate-To-Plate Garden

Old wooden crates are popular containers for culturing everything from spinach to strawberries. Not only are they an eco-friendly and inexpensive way to get gardening on your balcony, however they are also pretty space-effective.

Fresh veggies in wooden crates can also double as a striking decor in your balcony.

17. Tomato Balcony Garden

Why tomatoes? Well, they're easy to take care of and grow, they don't must much room, and they look loveliness, too.

But the best part is that homegrown tomatoes possibly used to make salads, sauces, and yummy tomato chutneys.

18. Hanging Wicker Baskets

While you'll employ pots of different materials to contain your vegetable yard, how about giving a try to hanging wicker baskets? Layer them with plastic, fill soil, and start <u>planting</u> veggies of your choice in them.

Idea: employ a woven wicker basket to store your balcony garden tools, equipment, seeds, and other supplies.

19. Vegetable Deck Garden

Transform your deck into a thriving vegetable garden. You'll fill up all the space with planters to maximize your yield. Leave simply a narrow passage in between for movement.

Idea: Make a small greenhouse for veggies that must more care to grow.

Apartment Balcony Garden Ideas

Give your tiny apartment balcony a green makeover. Sure you wouldn't be able to cultivate tons of vegetables and herbs in it, however you'll still live the garden life in limited space.

Here are some wonderful apartment balcony garden ideas for you.

20. Balcony Lawn

For an apartment-dwelling lawn lover, here's the perfect solution: Make a lawn feel in your small balcony employing <u>synthetic lawn turf</u>. this is easy to maintain and cost-effective.

Idea: Place a comfy swing chclimate, some potted herbs, and employ the space to unwind in the evening over a cup of coffee.

21. Jungle-Inspired Balcony Garden

A profusion of potted trees, lush herbs, and vines may transform your balcony into an enchanted forest. this can make a gorgeous statement that possibly noted from afar.

Plus, your balcony can get a sense of privacy, too.

22. Micro-Park Balcony

Supposing gardening means the world to you, you may as well employ every inch of space you have in your balcony. employ everything from clay pots and railing <u>planters</u> to hanging baskets and trellises.

It can give your balcony that mini-park look and make your gardening dreams come true even in a small apartment.

23. Rustic Apartment Balcony

You don't must tons of herbs to make a rustic statement in your balcony. A handful of potted herbs can also do the job. You'll essentially must containers and pots of varied sizes, shapes, and colors.

Arrange them randomly in your balcony and culture different types of herbs in them. You're sure to rock the rustic look.

24. Floral Oasis

For a blooming balcony that can make your space look warm and inviting, Make a floral oasis. How? Well, you'll herb sweet alyssum, begonias, geraniums, and petunias in colorful planters.

Idea: Take inspiration from the image below and spread a carpet of faux lawn grass for added effect.

Home Balcony Gardening Ideas

Starting your dream balcony garden at home? Give a go to vertical <u>planters</u>, hanging baskets, railing pots, and maybe even wooden crates.

Below are some great ideas you'll take inspiration from.

25. Cheerful Balcony Garden

How about a balcony garden overflowing with petunias and roses? Mount <u>planters</u> on the railing or hang them from the roof for an old-world feel.

For a bright and cheerful vibe, adorn your balcony with flowers in shades of reds, pinks, and yellows.

26. Balcony Corner Garden

Use a small corner of your balcony to culture herbs in. Line the railing with colorful planters and add a several freestanding pots and trellises to greenify your space.

Culture sunflowers, marigolds, lavenders, and fuchsias. Your petite corner garden is ready. Marigolds may even contribute to the repelling of mosquitos in your garden.

27. Repurposed Crate Garden

Make a raised flower bed in your balcony employing old wooden crates. They take up only a little space and are a clever and inexpensive way to culture herbs and vegetables.

Advice: Prevent your wooden crate from rotting by simply lining this with plastic.

28. Blooming Floral Garden

With a vibrant and colorful balcony, you'll make a dramatic statement even in a small space. Make sure you employ every inch of space you have. Culture herbs in hanging planters, rail pots, and even trellises.

Idea: Culture lots and lots of petunias in the shades of red and pink and employ ivy for a striking green contrast.

Vertical Garden Ideas for Balcony

Take advantage of the walls you have in your balcony. How? Simple, by vertical gardening! Hang pots on your walls employing trellises, shelves, and even gutters and pallets.

Take inspiration from these vertical garden ideas for your balcony.

29. Trailers herb Wall

Make a green waterfall in your balcony with trailing herbs in ceramic pots. Fix the pots to a clean wall employing metal or wooden holders.

Culture herbs like English ivy, golden pothos, string of pearls, and burro's tail and you're good to go.

30. DIY Pallet Hanging Garden

Upcycle old palettes for your vertical balcony garden. Fix this on a bare wall in your balcony and hang planters of different shapes and sizes on it.

This DIY project is budget-friendly and super easy to make. You'll simply source old palettes from small local grocery or retail shops.

31. Living Wall Balcony Garden

Dress up a barren wall in your balcony with leafy herbs of all shapes, shades, and sizes. this can give your space the needed depth and texture without taking up a lot of space.

Advice: For your living wall to thrive, make sure all the herbs in this have the same sunlight and water needs.

32. Colorful Vertical Balcony Garden

For a good splash of color, consider employing pots and herbs in vibrant hues. Polish a wooden palette to make this look more elegant and then hang orange, yellow, white, and green pots on it.

Next, herb flowering varieties like petunias and geraniums or culture herbs like dill and rosemary in your pots.

33. Balcony Trellis Garden

How about a painted trellis to hold your mini balcony garden? You may want to employ pots in dark shades of grey or brown. The arrangement can look uber minimalist.

Idea: You'll also introduce a box in your trellis, like in the image below. Fill this with soil and herb strawberries in this supposing you please!

Best Balcony herbs and Vegetables

You Dont must a huge backyard to cultivate herbs and vegetables. With the right container and herbs, you'll convert the limited space in your balcony into a thriving garden.

Best Veggies for Your Balcony Garden

Vegetables may add a little country charm to your balcony garden. Plus, culturing them organically means both good health and taste. You'll essentially must to do the same things you'll do in your backyard to culture them.

Some easy-to-culture balcony veggies are:

- Chives
- Radish
- Lettuce
- Beans
- Tomato
- Spinach
- Pepper
- Kale
- Potato
- Cucumber

Best Flowers for Your Balcony Garden

Bring flowering herbs to your balcony for a good summer vibe. Most herbs are easy to culture in planters. Still, you may want to stick with hardy herbs that may tolerate partial sun and survive drought.

Here are the best flowers to culture on your balcony:

- Petunia
- Fuchsia
- Rose
- Sweet Alyssum
- Pansy
- Geranium
- Hibiscus
- Salvia
- Hydrangea
- Marigold

How to Make a DIY Balcony Garden

Is your balcony in must of a little green? Get started on a DIY project for your balcony.

Whether you're a gardening pro or it's your first time at getting your thumbs green, you'll simply get started on this easy DIY balcony garden with our step-by-step guide.

Step one – Consider Your Space

Before getting your hands dirty, quite literally, take a close look at your balcony. See what direction this faces, the amount of sunlight this gets, and how much space you have.

That way you'll figure out what kind of garden to create.

Step two – Choose Your Design

There are endless design options you'll choose from. You'll go for railing [planters](), containers, herb pockets, vertical gardens, or a mix of these, depending on your space and taste.

Advice: Avoid hanging [planters]() supposing you live in a high-rise building. Supposing a pot fell off your balcony, this possibly really dangerous.

Step 3 – Choose Your herbs

Here's the fun part: choosing what you want to grow. You'll try a floral balcony garden to make your house look bright and blooming. Or you'll choose to get started on a more functional garden featuring herbs and veggies.

Whatever you decide, keep in mind the sun, water, temperature, and soil needs of your herbs.

Step 4 – Select Your [Planters]()

Balcony [planters]() should be compatible with the growth habits of the herbs you culture in them. For example, you'll must long and wide [planters]() for vegetables.

Advice: Make sure the [planters]() you fix on the rails are made of lightweight material like plastic.

Step 5 – Add Some Furniture

You probably want to employ the green balcony space to unwind when work. Maybe read a book or drink some tea there?

So don't forget to add to your balcony garden a couple of foldable chair, a lightweight swinger, or a mattress with some pillows.

Step 6 – Safety and Maintenance

Last however certainly not least, make sure all your [planters]() are securely fixed and won't tumble down with strong winds. Check also the weight restrictions you may have in your apartment balcony.

When this comes to maintenance, you'll have to ensure your herbs are being watered on time, they receive proper sunlight, and are pruned now and then.

Balcony Garden Frequently Asked Questions

Ready to Make a flora-filled garden in your own balcony? You may want to read through these important FAQs before you start dragging planters, crates, and trellises to your balcony.

What vegetables possibly grown on a balcony?

Almost every vegetable you'll culture in your backyard possibly grown in your balcony garden as well. Start with low-maintenance and easy-to-culture veggies like beans, green onions, peppers, eggplants, or cucumbers.

It's important that your vegetable planter is deep and wide and offers good drainage.

What do I must for a balcony garden?

Starting a balcony garden is quite easy. You'll must a balcony (obviously) that receives at least three hours of sunlight. Next, you'll must herbs or seeds, and some planters.

Finally, get your hands on basic gardening tools like a trowel, watering may, a pair of shears, etc.

How do I build a small balcony garden?

To build a small balcony yard, you'll first must to assess the space you have and how you'll employ this to the last bit. The rest is simple: bring in some planters and herbs and start gardening.

Less Is More

When this comes to gardening, sometimes **less is more**. You'll employ the small balcony space you have to culture herbs without a heavy investment of time, energy, or money.

With no lawn mowing or weeding, you'll have plenty of time to be creative. employ the space to culture herbs and vegetables and occasionally even host guests.

Only a bit of planning may turn your boxed-in balcony into a little Eden garden. And that too with minimal effort.

So, are you all prepped up to start your own balcony haven? allow **us famous in the comments section below!**

Until next time, happy balcony gardening!

Made in the USA
Middletown, DE
02 December 2020